(sub rosa)

(sub rosa)

Poems by Stan Rogal
Inspired by paintings by Jacquie Jacobs

Wolsak and Wynn ◆ Toronto

© Stan Rogal, 2003

All rights reserved. No part of this publication may be reproduced, stored in a retrieval system or transmitted, in any form or by any means, without the prior written consent of the publisher or a licence from The Canadian Copyright Licensing Agency (Access Copyright). For an Access Copyright licence, visit www.accesscopyright.ca, or call toll-free to 1-800-893-5777.

Typeset in Goudy Old Style
Printed in Canada by The Coach House Printing Company, Toronto.
Front cover art: "Bed" by Jacquie Jacobs
Cover design: Jacquie Jacobs and The Coach House Printing Company, Toronto
Author's photographs: Sid Tabak

Some of these poems have appeared previously in: *Murderous Signs*, *Kaleidoscope*, *Queen Streeet Quarterly*, *The Fiddlehead*, and *Rampike*, as well as in *The IV Lounge Reader*.

The publishers would like to thank the Canada Council for the Arts and the Ontario Arts Council for their invaluable support.

Wolsak and Wynn Publishers Ltd
192 Spadina Avenue, Suite 315
Toronto, Ontario
Canada M5T 2C2
www.poets.ca/wolsakwynn/

National Library of Canada Cataloguing in Publication Data
Rogal, Stan, 1950-
      Sub rosa / Stan Rogal; illustrated by Jacquie Jacobs
Poems.
ISBN 0-919897-87-8
I. Title
PS8585.0391S83 2003   C811'.54   C2003-901955-1
PR9199.3.R548S83 2003

Rose: A highly complex symbol; it is ambivalent as both heavenly perfection & earthly passion; the flower is both Time & Eternity, life & death, fertility & virginity. The rose also typifies science & secrecy, 'sub rosa', a rose being hung, or depicted in council chambers to symbolise secrecy & discretion.
 — *from 'An Illustrated Encyclopedia of Traditional Symbols'*
  by J. C. Cooper,

Fontenelle's rose saying that within the memory of a rose no gardener has been known to die.
 — *Diderot*

A rose is a rose is a rose...
 — *Gertrude Stein*

Contents

Preface	xi
Artist's Statement	xii
Colour Plates	xv
Sub Rosa	21
Sub rosa transformation: 1	23
Sub rosa transformation: 2	24
Sub rosa transformation: 3	26
Sub rosa transformation: 4	27
Sub rosa transformation: 5	29
Sub rosa transformation: 6	31
Paradise	37
Paradise transformation: 1	38
Paradise transformation: 2	40
Paradise transformation: 3	41
Paradise transformation: 4	43
Paradise transformation: 5	45

Frieze	49
Frieze transformation: 1	55
Frieze transformation: 2	58
Frieze transformation: 3	61
Frieze transformation: 4	63
Undone	67
Undone transformation: 1	69
Undone transformation: 2	73
Undone transformation: 3	74
Undone transformation: 4	76
The Haunt	83
The Haunt transformation: 1	84
The Haunt transformation: 2	86
The Haunt transformation: 3	87
The Haunt transformation: 4	89

Arrangement	95
Arrangement transformation: 1	96
Arrangement transformation: 2	97
Arrangement transformation: 3	98
Arrangement transformation: 4	100
Bond	105
Bond transformation: 1	107
Bond transformation: 2	109
Bond transformation: 3	111
Bond transformation: 4	113
Helix	117
Helix transformation: 1	118
Helix transformation: 2	121
Helix transformation: 3	123
Helix transformation: 4	125
Epigraph	126

Preface

In my poetry, I've tried to incorporate anything that would make the work rich, evocative and multi-layered. As such, I've always been intrigued with the notion of transformation and hybrid forms, both literally and metaphorically. I suppose this is why my poems often have a collage feel to them. I like to pull things from myths, fairy tales, pop culture, science, news articles, music, arts and so on, then toss in my own brand of sensibility and humour (puns, palindromes, nonsense…) in order to create pieces that are ripe with life on the page. I find that much of Jacquie Jacobs' work has a similar attitude and approach, especially her abstract figurative work, where the body always appears to be caught somewhere between human and plant or animal; between corporeal and ethereal; between real and imaginary.

Jacquie was living in Switzerland when she sent me the first photographed painting and asked me to write a poem for it. She wanted to make some postcards and perhaps even read the poem at her upcoming art show. I found the picture to be incredibly stimulating and decided to give her two or three poems to choose from. When she sent me a second picture I felt that there was the possibility for a collection of such paintings and poems, perhaps writing five or six poems for each painting. Not wanting to write a group of poems that were all the same, I tried to give myself a basic vocabulary in the initial poem and then transform the proceeding poems in various ways.

While this was a true collaboration in terms of fitting words to art, I never discussed with Jacquie what her ideas or thoughts were behind the paintings. At least at the outset, I wanted to be free of any influences beyond the works themselves and simply follow my own approach to them. I even asked Jacquie if I could change some of her titles to make them more suitable to my own purposes, and she readily agreed. Later, we did talk and it was fun and interesting to hear how our interpretations were similar or different. At this point, I did go back and make some alterations where I felt her 'take' was particularly cogent or useful.

It is our hope that readers of this book will also feel inclined to make their own interpretations of both the paintings and the poems.

We knew that the biggest problem for the book would be finding a publisher who would agree to print the paintings in colour, even though it made no sense (either for the paintings or for the poems) to show them in black and white. So, a big thank you to Maria and Wolsak and Wynn.

Stan Rogal

Artist's Statement

I enjoy working in a loose, collaborative way with artists in other disciplines: dancers, musicians, actors, writers. For the collaboration to work, there needs to be some shared sympathy for the subject matter and the style of expression. Different artistic personalities working through, or "riffing on," a mutually seminal theme is an exciting process to me.

Previously, Stan had used some of my sketchbook work to complement his poems and short stories, but the cross-pollination process was indirect. With the Sub Rosa series, I did the first painting, sent Stan a photograph of the work, and asked if he would be interested in writing a poem based on it. I wanted to produce some postcards with artwork and poetry together and was curious to see what Stan would come up with.

Because I was in Europe at the time that these paintings were done, I didn't discuss my ideas about them with Stan. This made his perceptions and writings even more of a surprise. I was delighted with our first collaboration and pressed him with more images, and he created more poems. The anticipation that occurred after I would send each image was exquisite, and it soon became clear to me that we were developing a manuscript. The sensual, intelligent, and humorous tone of Stan's writing eloquently pulled all sorts of new and intended associations to the fore of my work.

The first painting, titled the same as the series Sub Rosa, began as a small casein paint doodle (paint made from an ancient recipe consisting of yogurt cheese, ammonia and pigment powder), an experiment on plywood that kicked around the studio for a while. The image was later integrated into a larger oil on linen piece, finally completed, then carted off, still wet, to hang as one last piece for an exhibition in Switzerland.

Out of the eight pieces in the book, six are oils on canvas and two are "cutouts," paintings on irregularly cut plywood shapes. A ninth piece, also a cutout, appears on the cover. After the fact, these paintings seemed like narratives for myths, or dreams. Maria, at Wolsak and Wynn, has afforded us the amazing opportunity of presenting this collaboration in lavish colour, an honour indeed.

Jacquie Jacobs

a chance to say thanks to some of the many people who have directly or indirectly helped with this book:
Marina Bergamin, Helena Borody, Ingrid Buol, Silvia Buol, Glen Cadwick, Marie Charbonneau, Birgit Ciber, Drew Hauser, Roland Helmus, Constantin Jaxy, Amelia Jimenez, kleingallerie Muller, Klub Schule Migros Chur, KulturBrauerei Berlin, Molly Monahan, Maureen Paxton, Anja Rob & the Standardized Patient Programm, Ruben & Shirley Rivas, Mil Rufli, Jelena Sisic, Caroline Schmid-Skretteberg, Rudolf Stussi, Sylvia Sutter, Sid & Diana Tabak, Christipher Waldfielder, Claudia & Andy Zulig.

Special thanks to…
Stan Rogal,
Max & Errol Stussi,
Norma & Douglas Jacobs Sr,
Lilian Andree & Robert Schneider, Jill Battson

This is dedicated to the one I love.   –*The Mamas and Pappas*

COLOUR PLATES

Sub Rosa 17
oil on linen, 120 cm x 120 cm
In the collection of Stan Rogal, Toronto, Canada
Photo credit: Sid Tabak

Paradise 35
oil on linen, 120 cm x 140 cm
Photo credit: Christofer Waldfielder

Frieze 53
oil& pigment powder on wood, approx 110 cm x 85 cm
Photo credit: Jacquie Jacobs

Undone 71
oil on linen, 120 cm x 100 cm
Photo credit: Sid Tabak

The Haunt 81
oil on linen, 120 cm x 120 cm
In the collection of Andy & Claudia Zulig,
Lenzerheide, Switzerland
Photo credit: Silvia Sutter

Arrangement 91
oil & pigment powder on wood,
approx 110 cm x 85 cm
In the collecton of Lilian Andree, Basel, Switzerland
Photo credit: Jacquie Jacobs

Bond 101
oil on linen, 120 cm x 100 cm
Photo credit: Christofer Waldfielder

Helix 119
oil on linen, 100 cm x 100 cm
In the collection of Silvia Sutter,
Lenzerheide, Switzerland
Photo credit: Silvia Sutter

Bed (used on cover)
oil & pigment powder on wood,
approx 110 cm x 85 cm
Photo credit: Jacquie Jacobs

1. Sub Rosa

(sub rosa)

SUB ROSA

Beneath the rose begins a dark correspondence
As congress between the red lion & the white lily
Stretches one form toward the other.

Where primary appeal is to the eye
Nothing androgynous confuses, even with
Hair & nipples faded in the surgical light.

What suggests this eerie scape beyond the body's
Refusal to be disowned appears most unbecoming
& flesh adjusts to the comfort of its petalled spread.

In the swamp, tellurian seems to mate with itself,
Voluptuousness an issue wrapped in fluorescence
Making principles uncertain in respect to body limits.

Whether spurred by egg, bubble, oyster or moon
Desire for the hidden cause to be stripped naked
Remains a dream within a dream, dreaming.

Or that thing no human hand can touch
Without destroying renders each fantasy
Obsessive, & speculation turns to mirror gazing.

On the bank of the apocalyptic pool
The fiery red mandragora swells to monster fruit
Primed to spoon its bare reflection.

Omnia Munda Mundis: Unto the pure all things are pure.
Beating madder red from the inky night, the animal
Hybrid shifts at the jungled edge.

Taking the waters, who seeks travel with the whorl
Loses passport in the baser realm of matter.
Conception gone maculate where the juices temper.

The German proverb that states: 'a clear conscience
Provides the best pillow,' has the secret life of plants
Shift the hips to wonder.

SUB ROSA TRANSFORMATION: 1

What hoary secret whispers across the pitch
    to strike a body blooming?
What aloed tentacle seeks to balm the sanguine wound?
From any perspective
    hips shift & breasts heave to the cadence
                animal avidum generandi
Aristotle's beast greedy for generation
    hid in a fold of legs
        set to grind a child ecstatic.
Here is such livid music & such white light
That sparks a vessel madder red
    parting lips with the taste of Mandrake, love apple
        & every other nightshade
Magic.
Listen. The heartfelt noise of it.
The sound.

SUB ROSA TRANSFORMATION: 2

Where primary appeal is to the eye, nothing androgynous
Confuses. Beyond the aspect of chiselled flesh
Petals disclose to the ovulatory moon
Erecting a clime for vampires, werewolves & further incubi
    whose hot breath & hotter words threaten to nightmare
        this chaised habit
Fitful.
What might appear possession, instead
Embraces
    dizzy dreams, excited states, convulsive twitchings.
Spirit neither St. Vitus nor Asmodeus could bear to dance
More willing.
Here is *que sera, sera*
Arcanum
That belies transgression, figuring,
    at base, ruby fruit secretes a thick, volatile oil
        inclined to purge the staunchest beholder. Maculate
Christ or some other failed oyster
Hell-bent on palming thighs a madder red
A lifetime.

From the earth, illumination issues,
    & at each slippering heave, paradise prompts
        through ritual nakedness.
Takes to it.
Takes it to heart like no other.

SUB ROSA TRANSFORMATION: 3

On the bank of the apocalyptic pool
The fiery red mandragora swells to monster fruit
Primed to spoon its bare reflection.
Neverminding the cross
    between red lion & white lily
        meant to render any beast domestic
Here exists such grand aspect
    that might plumb the depths of whoreson wells
        advancing taste for the exotic.
'Rosebud' by any other name & smelling sweetly.
Just as an egg or a soap bubble, being substantial but
Delicate, cannot suffer the tenderest touch without
Bursting
    presents a form no rash few can resist.
Though this is mere woolgathering where
Who is most becoming emerges wholly
Naked
    almost nippleless, against the bombast.
Strange fruit grown comfortable in its earthly coil
Blooms immaculate in the glow.
Flourishes.

SUB ROSA TRANSFORMATION: 4

Watch and pray that ye enter not into temptation:
the spirit indeed is willing but the flesh is weak.
  — *Matthew 26:41*

What suggests this scape? What makes suggestive?
An outrage of petals? A whorl of fronds?
An oyster of pure, unadulterate light?
A moon that draws on blood fierce as any vampire?
A bubble of egg symbolising procreation & cultic promiscuity?
A figure prone to excess; to access —

                              venal, vernal, vernacular...

Displays:

    chirrup-chirrup grind of legs
    slippering *gurgle-purr* of hips
    rubadub-halloo roil of breasts
    racket of arms belling the ears
    mouth *huzza-hurrah* a vaginal cleft
    intoning enchantment
    perhaps sudden
    out-of-the-blue *yap-shriek* intercourse
    of sax & violins
    sacral *plash-clang* penetration of colour
    mainly: red, white, black

What might be made to situate the so-called consummate
Virgin/whore rushes all feeling to extremities.
'Beauty being in the eye; ear in the heart,' *et cetera...*
Makes plain Heisenberg's uncertain principles.
As before a mirror speculation begins & ends
    with the fatal brash image
        & *Shazam!* we behold what we want to behold.
Whether dazed & confused *auto-da-fé*
Romantic
Or some such other-
Wise driven Mandrake
Conjures variant
Autoerotic
Eve, on the one hand,
    her teeth & lips as yet undone by the love apple.
On the other, Sara, Asmodeus a bat up her ass
Prodding thrust & shove
Death
    of seven cardinal husbands.
Interpretation few dare entertain
Frames each digression an entrance
Long ago & far, far away.

SUB ROSA TRANSFORMATION: 5

Beating madder red from the inky sky, the animal
Hybrid shifts at the jungled edge.
What must be considered cause for some alarm
To any fatal voyeuristic
Rather, blinds with possibility:
    a mythology of recognition & revelation.
Faint hope
Whether stood downwind for no one good
Reason or another
    or snapping branches underfoot
        or merely settled in to rut from the periphery
Who refuse engagement amid the whirl
Bound to lose passport in the matter.
Total unfamiliar with the strangest phenomena
The glasses stop. They utter fail, yet, the image
Fingers somewhere back of the eye
Recollecting:
        a bat of light
        with power enough
        to spot the invisible.

No escaping this base materiality.
With everything so alive it can become almost anything
Primal water populates with nothing, save, transitional
Creatures.
At this fracture, skin crawls,
    hair bristles, ears & noses swell,
        high-pitched squeaks echo the landscape
Narrative bleeds through the marginals
Simply
& what was earlier obliged to contain all forms & aspects
        unwinds a body
        faceless
        & shrouded
        in fantastic
        petals.

Here is such bold relief that makes suggestive, or:
    the emergence as wild beast that comes so easily
        from the repressed, moves finally toward the cross.

SUB ROSA TRANSFORMATION: 6

Beneath the moon begins a bruised correspondence
As congress between the blue lion & the black lily
Stretches one form toward the other.
At this transgression exists an ear in the heart
That picks up what it wants to pick up
   (merely)
       through the infernal buzz.

> *Oh, sweet lunacy, come push to shove.*
> *Oh, rough crocodile of love.*

There are no mosquitoes at this picnic, thank Christ,
   & a rose is a reluctant vampire
      where a pearl harbours blood like
Nobody's business.
The mantis, however, threatens with its mandibular saw
& what might be taken as an open, friendly
Murmur
   might just as easily smack disaster.
Or, putting the pinch on,
   when the moon *halloos* a rainbow's arch design
      a seeming faultless 'V' of snow geese goes sudden bats.

Gravity's centre collapses while
    Soubrette suggests Sibyl in the beat drum, warning:
Sound the alarm, Marla!

> *Spurred by lips of johns & janes alike*
> *secrets become creatures on this darkling plain*
> *clamorous, hungered, hot &*
> *done to a turn.*

Where thunder is a rich source of loudness
Meant to shatter each blanket idyll
All hell cuts loose.
Listen — the body's flagrant sax & violins
Nature
    grinds to the raucous din.
Flesh swells, skin pricks, both Little Boy & Fat Boy
Peal out of proportion
    while Miss Enola Gay's atomic clit
        riddles the ear & heart of every shadowed
Moonstruck
On the lam
    & on the prowl.

> *Oh, sweet lunacy, come push to shove.*
> *Oh, rough crocodile of love.*

(paradise)

2. Paradise

Paradise

Where speculation equates mirror gazing
The faint fantasy of transformation slips beyond the frame
    & what appears most becoming
        emerges one stage steadily from another.
Creates a world younger, brighter & more perfect.
This, on the face of it, omitting:
        awash in this materiality, this material blushes aqua
        inviting otherwise visioned mermaids breaking surface
        for a taste of sun, shaking off gills & scales
        & shifting fins to flash in the plashy mud.
Such is the lure of otherness that compels the eye to look again.
Not necessarily daughters of Zion gathered at the river
Who walk with stretched-forth necks & wanton eyes
Making tinkling sounds with their feet.
Rather, nymphs, sirens, succubi arising from the pool
Half-formed, faceless, without nipples or pubic hair
Parting leaves in ritual nakedness
To set up a fall.
Or, taking the waters, invent a magic
To tease enchantment from the green-envy sky
        Then, with blue water tracing their shoulders
        Uproot, run through land where pigs, dogs, lions
        Leap to kiss their heels as they flash by.

Paradise transformation: 1

Figure '40 days & 40 nights' to spook a low ghost
Ark, or some such other miracle deliverance, whereas,
Nothing so settling within this frame
That favours every tension
Artificial.
Flood subsides & *maybe* the monsoon has passed.
Water gives way to distant shaky hills
    while sky breaks clouds into a greenish wash.
It is dark & it is light & it is neither &
    what multiplies by division in this scape
        rises luminous from the swamp.
Tectonic in aspect, a minor shift erupts
Transformation enough to rock the everyday
Fantastic.
Where gone naked in the stream begins the
Visions — blue mirage of brilliant
    foliage & brighter flesh grown latent with fatal promise.
Here records the fear of any mere man. The unconscious
Speaks to the unconscious
    tossing dust in the eyes, colouring any beauty
Suspect.

Whether Eve brooding a river of tears between her legs
Or unreal water-maidens with power to strip
& invert the order of things one can only imagine:
> Diana tethered to savage dogs primed to sic the most
> handsome curious.
> Lorelei lounged on a rock set to shipwreck the most
> avid adventurous.
> Our Lady of Lourdes bowed to heal the most
> awed fortuitous.
> Muses gathered to praise the most
> remote godliness & bring happiness to the wretched

Merely
Entrances a world
Ripe with blood &
Hung
    with abstracted possibility.

Paradise Transformation: 2

Astonish me.
Whether Logos or low ghost
   the word makes flesh any unholy trinity bent on
Salvation.
Here exists some base religious matter that bears remarking
& no amount of genuflect to ease the rapture.
As trembled before the sphinx gives cause to wonder:
        What mythic creature walks on four legs in the morning
          three legs in the afternoon & two legs in the evening?
No joke. The end gone-to-hell-in-a-hand-basket
   gets devoured by the toothsome maw.
How stand idly by & remain unamazed?
With everything leading unstopped toward the moment
& unable to step from the same river twice
   who cannot truly dream the blue flower any longer
      lies wrapt amid the filmy skin.
As caught up in the thick of it erects a notion.
Fronds part. Backdrop slips to wash.
Aquamarine alters bloodstone in the offering.
Sexual frankness enough to funk any beat heart.
Astonishes.

PARADISE TRANSFORMATION: 3

Form requiring the closest observation
Goes out with the weather.
Whether blue mirage
    or revelation of the secret self.
Whether crude burlesque of the risen dead
    or frankly decorative fantasy.
Whether comic mummers, murderous witches
    or the Fates playing out their tired old line:
        Clotho spinning, Lachesis judging length
        Atropos armed & ready with the scissors.
Whether *coup de torchon*
    or mere *fenestra* in the kneecap of history
Image ghosts past erasure, the fine dust filming the glass.
Call it life in death or death in life.
Such is the warp & woof, the morph of it that
Unshapes sudden emergence
Creatures
Half-mud, half-flesh arrested
    in various stages of ripeness
        at the recession of the flood.

Water being transitional mediates &
    little wonder
        reworks broke material.
But this is plain egocentric that
    begs the hidden cause to be stripped naked.
Or not.
Only much too much aware knowing
    when two see the same thing it is not the same thing
        proceeds regardless.
Look — how readily the new body is accepted!
No trick of flesh or freak of chance but
    strict determination delivers from the weeds.
Arrived at a place where
        better an impossibility that appears likely
        than a possibility that appears unlikely
The statues & effigies
Unwound
Seem on the point of walking.

Paradise transformation: 4

for Jacquie

Art being Nature's ape
    begins two metres distant from the body.
Whether Einstein, Plato or Circe
Form removes one state to another
    (as hirsute relatives, musical chairs or trained pigs
        serve to illuminate, lighting shadows on the cave wall)
Even as a painter
    (having never learned to disappear totally in the material)
Figures flesh outside the frame.
How put to rest this notion?
How know a shade of blue is blue?
Classic tits & ass
Model
    gone green in the green wood
        pose succulent, with powers enough,
            still, to put ghosts in heaven, gods in hell.
Makes a joke of broad strokes.
Here is enfolding of autobiographical fact, citing:
        "True beauty is unaware of itself."

Jacob's ladder or some such other
Ornamental clime that
    slips a tongue between the legs of *bona fide*
Historical.
Or, flipping the bird,
    when a chair is not a chair scrabbles somehow swinish.
Spells the shore with
    heady, brief enchantment in the bent light.

Paradise transformation: 5

Thought is a permanent orgasm
  — René Thom

Awoke though not awake
Edges blur, flesh turns opaque, all spread surfaces shine
As six inches of quiet rain snuggles in for a feel
Fingers
    somehow, somewhere, between the folds.
What comes from a night lit with wild abandon.
Johnny Walker Red or some such further blackguard
Excuse, arguing:
        'Deprivation of dreams impairs ability to manage reality.'
Yeah, sure.
This is the stuff of which...
    where bodies furniture visions &
        rule of thumb makes thought a permanent orgasm.
Whether inside or out this mechanical tapestry
Occurs the murmur —
    blue voices splashing naked in the turquoise wash
        lubricating the warp & woof, the nap, the weft & wale of it.

Though at a point of least resistance
    (& for no one good particular weave or another)
        fabric twists almost tectonic in its alarm, the entire scene
Spooking
   laid to waste
       before passion's passing bell.

(frieze)

FRIEZE

> *Roses must grow between their lips.*
> *— Virginia Woolf*

What horizontal
strip
laid flat & plain
as any
shaggy nap
that
marks a freeze
a gliff
of ornamented
woollen cloth
coarse with bodies
sucking
warp & woof
weft & wale
marrow
from the
rose.

What division
of entablature
richly sculpted
that
presents such
frankly
decorative fantasy
why, in this
tiny corner
of the Cosmic Sodom
one might expect
the still stale
odour
of pears
a vagrant hand
sudden
striking
up a smoke
a tray with
buttered clams
long brooded
among grapes

of spent intercourse
shedding shells
& come
whistling up their
sleeves

or the petals
spread *just so*
as lips
in some ripe
fashion
promise
ever
& ever
& ever

3. Frieze

FRIEZE TRANSFORMATION: 1

Hardly Tabula Rasa
as even in repose
bodies fill the surface
& colour fills the bodies.
What else, meaning
If clear conscience
provides the best
pillow, then...?
Instead groan restless
in the jungled sheets
whether chased by or
in chase of something
(some *thing*)
'lions & tigers & bears,
oh my.'
Monkeys also, all so
done in by the tear
& scratch of chronologic.
Done in by REM.
Done in by alarm.

Done in by a slight girl
with concussed skull
& ruby slippers.
Little Red or Briar Rose.
How lay content
with so much
infernal buzz?
This is some Zodiac, eh,
that lacks a single solid star
to hitch one's wagon;
that pitches in the dark
& offers little else but
hollow drums, empty straws
fraidy cats & broken wind
to set the locomotion.
How commit to a plan, a
pattern, a human intercourse
that always changes
never lasts, never becomes
affectionate?
Tattooed in the bone
fashions memory a
massage, where,

airing on the side
love broadcasts its *too-too*
familiar refrain:
"Over the Rainbow"
"Happy Together"
"Your Cheatin' Heart"
or other similar
beyond the grave
predilections.

FRIEZE TRANSFORMATION: 2

Who sings
the body electric
anymore
except by
measured ground
plugs the hole of
each fine-tuned
instrument
set to swell
past midnight
portraits in jazz
air on the side
excess conducting
both lean & cool
fanged & woolly
across the wire
as blue notes &
pear-shaped tones
groan
a scratch of roses
between covers
the buzz blooming
each ribald naked

sound
cheating left of centre
to the main vein
& laying low
horizontal bop
the rabble roused
plucked & blown
drummed & fingered
to shaggy nap
or shocked
high infidelity
hankering a groove
the hungered heart
sparking cats to prowl
chicks to wander
for a taste of sax & violins
horn & snare, a snarl of
stripped bodies
parting petals with their teeth
tension baldly welting surface
in the riff

here lies wit, man, that
waltzes free & easy
amid the dross
whether
light rock
country shlock
or pop
surely
bolts
against the current.

FRIEZE TRANSFORMATION: 3

Flesh marks
according to the scratch
according to the tooth
& nail of it
tiger country, perhaps
perhaps a cave drawing
perhaps the stuff of
legends
paused to the max
the ripe fruit bruising
roses in the clinch
what bouquet claws
the senses so
& thrashes either
joy or pain equally
also presents a gliff
which startles
the thornbush, say,
that speaks only by
bleeding
through the gash

in its trunk,
or the words of lovers, say,
gushing simply
across the pillow
between the sheets
hot tiger breath
still rough upon the neck.

FRIEZE TRANSFORMATION: 4

Rats live on no evil star

Why is a rose that turns
as primrose alters promiser
at the bud
as gliff sounds glyph
suggesting a fright
a picture glimpsing
itself
bent
in the bent light
as frieze hotly teases
a horizontal strip
toward a coarse
woollen cloth
iced
with shaggy nap
as no lemon no melon
spins forever
forward & back
the same still stuff
as this 'why'

divines a wishbone
in the heart
as any rose unfolds
Eros from the petals
bending flesh to spoon
in the night's dark
quiver
as ah, rose becomes
a horse one desires
to mount
& gallop to the ends
of the earth
returning
& returning
& returning

(undone)

UNDONE

Guess who
    rendering the scene a pulse
        goes noumenal in the gloss.
At back, uranium lilts the lunar sea madly
Erotic, while foreground teases optic
Warp & woof
Cause
    for abstraction enough
Neverminding

        she's come undone
        didn't notice that the light had
        changed

As here & there the beat & flicker tends bodies
Toward dissolve.
Ah, that old bordello moon altering love's bright
Promise, dances light to its light way
    & fashions figures abstract that move abstractly
        naked not nude, recalling 'we shoot nudes'
Emerges
    both reconciled & estranged amid the bud.

now it's time to rearrange

What might mistake a melon slice or drinks on a tray
Remains, otherwise, fairly constant:
    phosphor bronze catch of legs, ass, belly, breasts
    some snatch of *mons veneris*
    sweet aureole of nipple sounding out the mix
Portrays exotic in the clime.
Candy for any eye or ear
That serves to pound a steady line
Perverse, as:
       'The apparition of these faceless in a cloud.
        Petals spent on wet, black boughs'
Makes mutable

    light changed
        rearranged
            she's come undone.

UNDONE TRANSFORMATION: 1

Blinded by the light goes pop. Sparks a
Hunka-hunka, love, say, or some further
Burning
    in flagrante delicto.
At once substantial & indefinite
The mechanical universe presents
A vessel of smoke & mirrors
    darting bare-assed for the hills.
A deuce sporting horned shades & sulphurous *do*
    snaking brazen into the clearing.
Or, stood resolute in the wings
An other
    strange & wondrous
Naked.
If myths are the genitals of the collective unconscious
Goes pop amid the culture.
Unable to dream the blue flower ever again
Without half imagining:
    here, there, now, you, me...
Flesh melts, the mouth breaks like an egg.

Fracture remains constant even as approach shifts
    & a nipple of memory signals
        the single *mumblemumble* hook:
'Dressed up like a douche,
        Gonna roll her in the night.'

4. Undone

UNDONE TRANSFORMATION: 2

Who seek travel within the whorl
Lose passport in the baser realm of matter.
Club Med gone crazy in the heat
& how Art blurs the line
Reforming
    stark tits & ass
        to meaner shape & colour.
Dreams no longer a clear blue expanse
Where dysfunction of a mind
    makes for some strange & astonished
Here, now,
The manner in which the light hangs
Just so.
A trick of flesh with ability to move one to
Terror; the object itself
    seeming to dissolve
        amid a field of moot relations.

UNDONE TRANSFORMATION: 3

In vogue.
Here. There. Now.
Where the noumenous is creaturely presence
    presents further adventures in the skin trade
        hanging loose & looking like a million.
Being unaware or unconcerned that to be transformed
Is no longer to exist
Ambient American breed gone south for the weather
Pose

    bend me, shape me, anyway you want me...

Such is the catch &
    what sparks an infatuation with superlatives
        leaves little room for recovery of the ordinary.
Whether UV index, a rework of broke material
   or a case of muscle dysmorphia makes burlesque, baby.
Wave & particle, particle & wave flame alchemical as hell.
Bodies alter
    & both beach guys & beach gals shift
Perverse in the perverse light.

Who got the power...?
Witness a golden ass flicker the burning bush.
Illumination issues with no resort to roses for a sudden
Disfiguration.
Only, hung up on the buzz:

> *So long as you love me, it's all right.*

Undone transformation: 4

> *These faces are without sex, they have brooded among*
> *ghosts of passions till they have become ghosts themselves.*
> *— poet Arthur Symons commenting on the art of Simeon Solomon*

Barely off-tropic
Who are not long familiar with the strangest phenomena
Barely recollect, save through
    been there, done that, bought the T-shirt, cha, cha, cha
        cheap postcards, peeling skin, faint
            aroma of coconut oil or lingering *la turista*.
'Our lady of the Iguanas' being only somewhat otherwise
Even Art, her sigh man, her side man
Stroking sacral
    red, white, black against the shifting scape
Cannot endure.

> *Fade away & radiate*
> *Fade away & radiate*

Essentially a comedy, except it ain't funny.
Memory cooled to a point of mere wonder
    wonders why the universe bothers to exist at all?

Tide high & moving
    debris goes hairy on the blonde-out beautied beach
        where surf, sand & vegetation appear to merge.
Sun blooms a white rose on the shoulder sparking flesh
Electric
As bodies, too,
    (being no less than smoke & mirrors)
        pulse & beat, beat & pulse
End their brief design.
As on this desperate flight
    (tide high & moving)
        raises a chill at over 30,000 feet.
Vessels burst &
    faces without sex brood among ghosts of passions
        till they become ghosts themselves.

>*Fade away & radiate*
>*   Fade away & radiate*
>*   Cha, cha, cha...*

(the haunt)

5. The Haunt

THE HAUNT

a transformation of a fragment of a piece by Aaron Shurin

Fool! Who has merely to extend a hand
To effect contact with the landscape.
It's the gentlest tone in an otherwise haunted nature —
    brown & orange greeting the advances of cobalt & red.
Standing ground conveys by colour & shape
In which the most obvious is posture. One figure so
Apart the common manner, two others spread in courteous
Design: bold, blue hydrangeas
                splashed against the green grotto wall.
Fool! What strange resolution that chills a heart with a look
Renders paradise a blue mirage
Ghosting image
After image
Gone

THE HAUNT TRANSFORMATION: 1

There are strange gatherings. The two weird sisters naked
   in the pool, one rolling her tits, the other her ass. Flaunting it.
The guard naked. Unallowed to flaunt it. His member in escrow,
      under threat of... et cetera.
You've heard the story a dozen times. You've read the book.
You've seen the movie. You've bought the T-shirt.
Think John Travolta jerking off Pulp Fiction & barely making it.
You know, the one about the guard, the two weird sisters
(OK, Diana & her entourage, daughters of the King, mafia moll,
   whatever else variant...)
Naked.
Common sad story with similar fate. Countless unfortunate
Fallen
   at the sight: two weird sisters, naked, putting on the tease,
     twinned eternal in their passioned
               blood's bright offering.
Otherwise everything was brilliant.
Sky. Leaves. Water. The graceful slope of hills
Breaking into trees.

For someone with a bent for watching paint dry
    a moment's rest
        toward the inevitable
Execution
Seemed to beg pardon.
Or, wishing himself a reed among other reeds
Simply snaps, floats off in the distant distance
Beyond reach.
Beyond recall.

THE HAUNT TRANSFORMATION: 2

In the swamp, tellurian seems to mate with itself
Voluptuousness an issue rapt in fluorescence
Making principles uncertain with respect to body limits.
As to how one enters, naked or otherwise,
Drives home the point — necessary or sufficient?
Neither necessary nor sufficient?
Awash in this materiality
    myth dissolves
        in a desire to fit, flesh
Roots
All its worth.

THE HAUNT TRANSFORMATION: 3

A fair thought
    to lie between maids' legs.
Where nothing comes of nothing
Hamlet
    (centuries composed at the water's edge)
Remains a further fateful naked dead
    among naked dead, open to the haunt.
        Hey, non nony, nony, hey nony...
For all the withered matter:
    crown of pansies roiling the brain pan
    rosemary an albatross around the neck
    musty odour of long-since-faded
                        fennel, columbine, rue
Somehow twigs 'remember me' through the blue funk. Here is
Sight for sore eyes that conjures Ophelia's bare reflection
Ghosting double in the stream, appearing ripe enough
To transform this place
    of madness, murder, rape
        to one of bucolic, splashy pleasures.

Who is aroused by such will to tease the possible, stands yet
Uncertain on the rocks, no sudden man-to-Mandrake
Convert
    set to root magic from the deadly night shades, but,
        human, all too human, seems. Where doubt exists
Image pales & conscience fashions cowards of us all.
No death here, no sleep, simply the dream
Within the dream, dreaming itself
A lifetime.

THE HAUNT TRANSFORMATION: 4

With kind thoughts to M.C. Escher

What makes wilderness perfect is most becoming.
As bodies, also, belonging
    both to air & water are most becoming
        though unable to escape their own hot press
Flash
Stark naked for all the world.
Strike a pose of breasts, buttocks, oyster cream
    thighs
        while raking salamanders from their coal black manes.
Small wonder they'd next transform to birds.
Or fish.
Or nocturnal moths fluttering about tombstones.
Or witches high on smoking the devil's dick
    conjuring
        Walpurgis Night for eternity.

But this is just plain egocentric
Fingering
    who seeks to warp artless nature
        whorific
            is charged full by what he lacks.

Rather wish stones to bark
Or horns to sprout his own tangled scalp.
Not generally mean-spirited but somehow *out of joint*
For sake of an inability to utter sounds of love
Tongue turns to mud, lips slip
& the brain
    (being the most erotic organ in the body & least appealed to)
Trips over its two left feet
Stumbles so far from the clutch as to drive any vision
Bats.

What might at a glance appear to be
    a not-so-rosy picture is, as well, most becoming.
Bird got to swim. Fish got to fly.
Woman got to flower & hope for the best.
You can lead a ghost to water.

6. Arrangement

(arrangement)

ARRANGEMENT

Every dream is a repressed desire
— Sigmund Freud

What telepathy that orchestrates behind the bloom & renders mind a virtual playground for every vagrant image? Whether tower, shoe or sprawl of roses begins the cycle, as the hallucinatory quality of the actual shifts one bright object toward another. How buttonhole such conflagration once admitting: 'If one accepts the punishment for it, one can allow oneself the forbidden thing.' Being in & of the moment merely buckles in the clinch, the train speeding, the tunnel widening, the instruments of pain & pleasure a faint bogey in the distant distance.

Arrangement transformation: 1

What dissolves the marriage bed beyond the faded bloom, beyond whatever's gained or lost by steady compromise, beyond the making do with less or the putting up with more, beyond the give & take, beyond the lies & half lies, beyond glossing virtue a necessity, beyond having to make the best of being dealt a bad hand or grown bored with being dealt a good hand, beyond the failure to communicate, beyond the house, the car, the bills, the RSP's, the life insurance that costs an arm & a leg & bets that you live, beyond the kids, the friends, the family, the dog, the cat, the toilet seat up or the TV volume down or crumbs in the orange juice container or wet towels in the dirty wash basket or the toothpaste squeezed from the middle of the tube

beyond the slings & arrows of outrageous fortune

beyond this & that & whatever else *everyday*, ends, finally, at the vision gone under cover of the rose that dreams to flush the eviscerate form with animated flesh upon flesh. Here occurs such strange juxtaposition that lays a sword in between while simultaneously haunts the sheets with a wrestle of dragons. What beauty! What heart's desire, purling, 'Do that again. Then do the other thing,' settles satisfaction by action in the dawning, the glasses shattered, the rose stem snapped in a clench of teeth, the cigarette dangled at the lip, as beyond this light fantastic, *the world goes on & on its petty pace*, gravely figured & blindly pitching in the dark.

ARRANGEMENT TRANSFORMATION: 2

What panic discovering bodies recompose every seven years shifts the mind to matter. Air goes florid amid the bump & grind that grays anatomy toward disintegration, the flower barely taking hold before the petals lacklustre droop & drop. Here is such cheap horror that ghoulish bruises flora to fauna in the mix, the hunchback buttonholed to the grave, the evil genius turned nosegay in the current electric fry. On the spot, music pulses melodious then macabre as shadows stake the moon & beards sprout the limbs of trees. At centre of this misadventure must be a force which seeks to express something & still another equal ghostly which strives to prevent its expression. You know, the one about the crazed botanist seeking a cure for cancer but hatching a Frankenstein from the bloom instead & who ends the greater monster? Such is the course of natural history that fails to identify but alters willy-nilly through the fume. As nipped in the bud relays synapse to synapse against the flow or deadhead encourages a shoot or bare fact that human skin accounts eighty percent of house dust leaves an audience withered & screaming at the root.

Arrangement transformation: 3

What passes for love amid the spread makes for some strange couplings & stranger copulations. Neverminding the cucumbers, the cored apples, the peeled grapes, the lychee nuts, the artichokes or the melons gone lemons. Neverminding the oils, the unguents, the body paints, the edible panties, the raw eggs oozed into cracks or the oatmeal enemas. Neverminding the German shepherds, the greased pigs, the KY sheep, the airborne monkeys, the funky chickens or the plastic fantastic lovers. Neverminding the ropes, the chains, the handcuffs, the silk gags & leather belts, the boots, the cock rings, nipple rings, labia rings, the velvet swings, the horsehair underwear, the bishop outfits or the pussy whips. Neverminding the creamed jeans, the boob lubes, the polished puds, the pearl necklaces, the golden showers or the coprologics. Neverminding the neoprene vaginas or the ceramic studded dildos. Neverminding the soft music, the wine, the oysters, the chocolate truffles, the mary jane or the stain of *steak tartare* bled across the teeth. Neverminding the pumped up promises, the lousy poetry, the dirty words or the cunning lingo. Neverminding the things that enlarge, that reduce, that engorge, that expel, that nip, tuck & fold, that suck & blow, that swallow or the things that go bump & grind in the night. Neverminding Kama Sutra, Qi-Gong, Cosmic Yoga, *roman à clef*, fire breath, around the world, rim shot, butterfly, side mount, doggy style, mudslide, missionary with a twist, 69 or every otherwise constellation.

Neverminding blind desire for the blonde, adolescent cheerleader with the Pepsodent grin & the American Beauty crotch, the high school quarterback with the razor-blue eyes & the goal post *derrière*, the girl guide cookie, the boy scout wolf, the acne-scarred pizza delivery guy, the buck-toothed waitress, the halitosis hunchback or the butt-ugly concupiscent who can fart the entire Beethoven's Fifth while giving head to a six-pack of ding-dongs.

Neverminding all of this & more is played for laughs against the real perverse. Bodies so couched beneath the weight of roses that blood runs cold & any untoward *stimulus response* appears cause for alarm that sets teeth on edge & tumbles love arse-over-tea-kettle out of favour.

Arrangement Transformation: 4

Surrealism is the business of poets who cannot benefit from Surrealism.
 — *Jack Spicer*

What kick of covers that upsets an arrangement, whether eviscerate flesh or roses pinned to buttocks, barely raises a whelp in this still conflagration. Where a further flower might brood a face, a garland stretches a litter, petal upon mongrel petal: yellow, ochre, red, dogging the landscape. Ockham's razor aside, at issue, associations present when focussing on portions separately. As regression to primitive mechanism tells us bodies are the furniture of dreams exhaling pillows from the cheek, or Surrealism is a coat of many collars. At this illumination, (figuring Freud exist or not), the unconscious speaks to the conscious, the clinkered pack bitched with love & longing left howling at the moon.

7. Bond

(bond)

BOND

At edge, heart is a lonely haunter
Low ghost
    tempered to no-good diabolic.
Nothing translates here.
Whether dusk or dawn; the fair ones rising or sinking.
A bird takes wing in the background
    though it's hardly the same ectoplasmic:
        bird, plant, rock, angel, apparition, *thing*.
What begins as scant desire, say, a fleeting glimpse
    remains somehow open to suggestive.
Remark or otherwise chaste p-o-v made flesh.
This is perspective bent in the bent light.
As pleasure of the text astonishes with its
    come hither look
        that spoons each base principle
Uncertain.
With everything so alive it can become almost anything
Familiar breeds content. Arouses spirits leeching
    here, there, now, you, me... one form toward another.
Dooms whatever measured & scaled body entering the scene
To travel
    trance to trance to trance to trance... *eternal*.

Or, hard upon the scent, a fire bush (sudden) churns the waters
    spooking the general area awash in fatal flames.
Here, what might be considered means to magic
    that conducts the sexual initiation of the hero, instead,
        feints ghoulish, draws a dark *hello* around the dark skull.
Barks into the coppery heaven.

BOND TRANSFORMATION: 1

Dusk. It is no accident that
    sun cedes to the forces of darkness.
This is precisely the point
              where animal nature comes to play.
As Milton's Lucifer fared as well
Spiralling the wormhole only to re-emerge
    none the worse for wear
        sleek, scaled & embraced within the garden walls.
As here, the dragon tree shrouds in fantastic wings
Bellows its blood message
    purging pure blue sky to phosphor bronze.
Racoons dislodge from rooftops, bats keen, slugs
    draw their eerie glyphs across the vegetative ground
        adulterous mice murmur the adulterous wood
            while owls sport with the invisible.
Humans, too, go soft focus, shed their grim skins
For a taste of earthy pleasures.
A man (husband?) swan dives one end of the lake.
Closer by, a woman (wife?) moistens at the sight
    of a tall, cool glass of water
        lurking camouflaged in the bush.
What might normal contract a marriage, instead

Boxes shadows
    the each jerking the other
        with teasing glances & trash talk whispers
Along with all other kind lewd activity
Distance dissolves with the light
Frolics.

BOND TRANSFORMATION: 2

> *Ever love a psychopath, an individual void of*
> *conscience, incapable of grief? [Yeah, me too.]*
> — Judith Fitzgerald

From whose p-o-v?
What must necessarily be regarded as comic
Relief to some
Fabricates a map of further
    erections & disasters for others.
Whether Isis or Diana naked for all the world
Bound to catch an admiring eye or two
    though who might barely act on this charmed scene
Ends
    barking up the wrong tree.
Is this a threatening gesture or what?
Knowing a twig swell with sap has little chance
    amid the more common rooting
        is still hard pressed to leave-take.

At this intrusion, to lend a koan
Makes pretty volatile
Almost lyric:
    'Oh, the lady's gone moist...'
Seeming reason a'plenty to judge dismemberment
In this tight knit club
Where dragons palm the moon for sheer
Pleasure
    & amid the general slapstick
        assorted limbs fly off in all mean direction.

BOND TRANSFORMATION: 3

Curiouser & curiouser, sighs Alice.
Feeling the hole moisten at the lip of the pool
    a hair's breath fingers a slippering slip &
        D
            O
                W
                    N
                        she
                                  goes...

Heisenberg's uncertain principles aside
When love gets too vanilla why deny the self
Illusions?
As on the wing
    one draft makes her higher, one draft higher still.
Go ask Alice!
Who has scant desire to sleep with virgins
To test one's vow of celibacy
    rather tumbles in the dragon's palm
        oozing thick & oily through the gash.
What faint surrealistic

Can desire to pillow against the roar, where
    (in the dead of night)
        blackbird sings
            barkish figures beetle into shadows
                all kind animal mimics one mouth unto
An other?
I mean, how interpret such cunning linguists
Except as plastic fantasy?
Except as vitriol humour?
Except as lovers *a'buzz* in the offing
    swapping spit
        & shedding skins to moon the panorama?

White rabbits included, time holds no special place
    but, ticks off, in general.
As (meanwhile), sky bottoms out
                        & the good ship Icarus
Plunges.
Sets each available liquid
Blazing.

BOND TRANSFORMATION: 4

What amount of change to trip the light
Fantastic?
Even fully aware that innocence provides success
    where magic is the key
        must still stumble at the fact:
                Love is a wound inside the body, baby,
                & unrequited love, a bore.
Yet, whether hoodoo, klieg or comet's tale
Sky blushes indigo to chestnut & the *all too-sound* stage
Erupts.
Here begins stark impression against the night's demise
As radio activity rather jams the dumb perspective with
Dumb lyrics & dumber tunes spun classic by an age, like:

        In the misty moonlight, by the flickering
        Firelight...

For what reason? To what end?
Legs sudden kick up all their worth, demure eyes shift
Wanton
    & flesh grown former barkish at the edge
        now *hellos* across the flash in true Cartesian swell.

No mind, no matter, no matter what
                          here, there, now, you, me...
Dances
In the clearing Hell, oh:

> *Everything is all right, so long as you are*
> *Near...*

(helix)

HELIX

Constellation Gemini: the twins.

With moon a rose in the saturnal house
    & what suspends in the glacial drift, namely:
Clay, silt, sand, finely divided rock particulate, bone
Heavenly bodies
    or some other feint glass
        astride the oyster's back.
A form like a screw thread winding fathom upon fathom.
A trick
Of flesh eating disease
    meant to illustrate gray
        anatomy against the bluish floe.
Whether storm-tossed or
    the recurved border of the external ear
Drops a line:
            in flagrante delicto.
Here accounts the nicest incest
    that witnesses the enfolding of autoerogenous fact.
At this point, heat index bumps out of proportion.
Positions missionary
Turned
    tail & rut in the slippering fume.

HELIX TRANSFORMATION: 1

Constellation Pisces: the fishes.

Being the last sign of the Zodiac & closely bound
With the symbolism of water &
Dissolution
Whips Neptune screwing shapes of
    man, woman & fish to
        further mermen & mermaids
            gone frenzied 'round his trident.
What ball of confusion that marks both
Beginning & end to passion.
Whether failed 69 or some such other *auto-da-fé*
Amid the froth & spume
    bodies thrash in polar opposition.
Friend Kierkegaard's fear & trembling to the point
Merely raises heat at the shift of this icy-blue leap.
Where failure to situate stares straight into the moon's eye
Madness becomes part & parcel with the rest.
At this insistence, vision of a white rose
Backs a vomit of stars & across the shadowy drift
An act of faith spirals poor, cold fish to their knees
    the promise of Phoenix
        rising
            pie-in-the-sky from ashes.

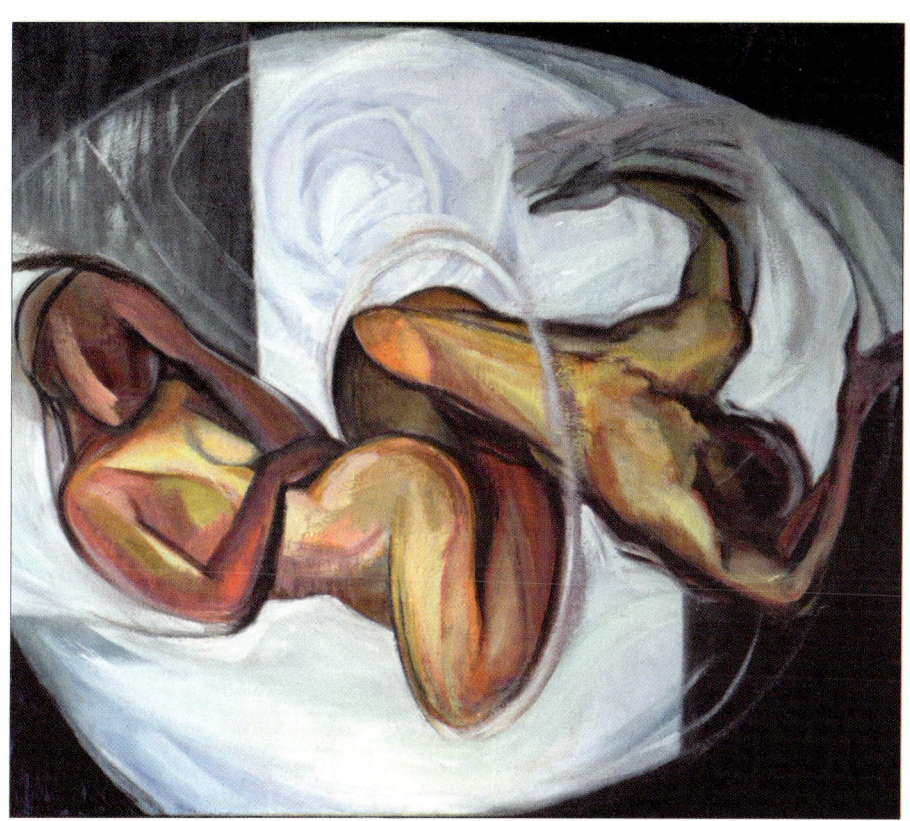

8. Helix

HELIX TRANSFORMATION: 2

Constellation Aries: the ram.

Following the thread, horns split &
    the sweet milt of Pisces' bolt impulses
Potential to actual.
Here fathoms beginning without end
Butting heads in some gross manner.
As at the heart, an ear recurves wholly
External to the beat & rale.
What of it?
'All things flow' said some Greek, & made stone
Dead now for some time (for all time, methinks,
    flowing).
Meanwhile, outside the window, (though not
    outside, but beyond)
Glaciers
    maintain their steady drift
        drip their milky stream of suspended particulate.
Exanimation occur or not occur.
Is that a question?
At this juncture (flow or no), ozone buoys Club-Med

Pigmentation darkens &
Wurm turns tail.
This is neither astronomy nor poetry nor business
This is science
Wondrous &
    what utter surf
              crashing.

Helix transformation: 3

*Forget about the psychological mechanism & let
the unconscious speak to the unconscious.*
— Richard Wagner

Constellation Cancer: the crab

Not so much numeric as symbolic
Presupposes
The Yin & Yang of it.
Still, scrabbling sidewise against the floe
Soft-shell tends to 69 in the crush.
Or, across this frozen sheet
Wound
No unidentified flying objects but real
Heavenly bodies
    sent to mediate the formal & informal
        worlds
            with their heated intercourse.
Where a slotted screw might serve as well
How rate the pen mightier than this word
    H-e-a-v-i-n-g
        seven letters upon the triple score?

At this threshold (with rose a blank tile in the moon's
Frieze)
Aspect turns grave
    's mythology inside out.
Whether lead to lead or lead to gold
Bawdy language sparks saturnalia in the criss cross
Eating its own tale.

Helix transformation 4

Constellation Aquarius: the water bearer

Under bent back & thrashing all he's worth
What flood raises ghosts from maculate bed sheets
    enough to bolt a man
        whereas this other settles easy in the gray matter?
Beyond Eve brooding a river of tears between her legs.
Beyond dreams & nightmares.
Beyond the worm's mad burrow.
Beyond smoking the devil's dick.
Beyond Hitchcock blonde betrayal.
Beyond ebb & flow.
Beyond *deus ex machina*.
Beyond noumenal glow.
Beyond what *seems*.
Beyond screw threads.
Beyond abstraction.
Beyond the pleasures of the text.
Beyond the names of the rose.
Beyond a taste for Mandrake.
Beyond the fiery red mandragora.
Beyond mirror speculation.
Beyond the magic of *Shazam!*

Beyond the rough crocodile of love.
Beyond Logos or low ghost.
Beyond these faces in a crowd.
Beyond human, all too human.
Beyond blood's bright offering.
Beyond *fade away & radiate.*
Beyond Miss Enola Gay's atomic clit.
Beyond white rabbit & surrealistic pillow.
Beyond *here, there, now, you, me...*
Beyond warp & woof, wale & weft.
Beyond either necessary or sufficient.
Beyond Heisenberg's uncertain principles.
Beyond Aristotle's beast greedy for generation.
Beyond the design of bold, blue hydrangeas.
Beyond fear of 69 or saturnine
    or Mercury's winged oyster flesh.
Beyond Tectonic shift or glacial drift
    or the moon's bruised phases.
Beyond the slings & arrows of outrageous fortune.
Beyond Ourobouros in love with its own tail.

Beyond & above & beside it all
   legs fold under a perfect ass, shaping a perfect
     vaginal cleft
        into which a man might either sink or swim.
Into which a man might either shun or embrace.
Here it all begins. Here it all ends.
The ever liquid
Flowering.

Mallarmé stressed the importance of not describing directly, precisely or exactly his subject, but of evoking & suggesting it. He emphasised the importance of the sounds of words & their musicality.
  — from 'Symbolists & Decadents' by John Milner